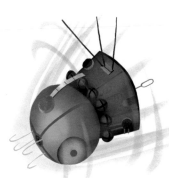

IMAGINE YOU WERE THERE...

WALKING ON THE MOON

IMAGINE YOU WERE THERE...

WALKING ON THE MOON

CARYN JENNER

KINGFISHER
LONDON & NEW YORK

KINGFISHER
LONDON & NEW YORK

Copyright © Macmillan Publishers
International Ltd. 2019
Published in the United States by Kingfisher,
175 Fifth Ave., New York, NY 10010
Kingfisher is an imprint of Macmillan
Children's Books, London
All rights reserved.

Distributed in the U.S. and Canada by Macmillan,
175 Fifth Ave., New York, NY 10010
Library of Congress Cataloging-in-Publication data
has been applied for.

Series editor: Elizabeth Yeates
Illustrations: Marc Pattenden (Advocate Art Agency)
Design: Dan Newman
Cover design: Laura Hall
Consultant: Carole Stott

ISBN: 978-0-7534-7500-3

Kingfisher books are available for special promotions and
premiums. For details contact: Special Markets Department,
Macmillan, 175 Fifth Ave., New York, NY 10010.
For more information, please visit: www.kingfisherbooks.com
Printed in China

9 8 7 6 5 4 3 2 1
1TR/0319/WKT/UG/128MA

Picture credits: 6-7 bg
NASA; 8bl CBW/Alamy; 9tr
Rockatansky/iStock; 9br
Mega Pixel/Shutterstock;
12b Historical/Getty; 23bl
(waiting on credit); 27c Henrique
Alvim Correa; 27cr Henri de
Montaut; 31t NASA/JPL-Caltech;
39tl (waiting on credit); 42
Image Science and Analysis
Laboratory, NASA-Johnson
Space Center; 54-55 NASA/
GSFC/Arizona State University;
58-59 bg 3DSculptor/iStock;
58t jamesbenet/iStock; 58b
gremlin/iStock; 60-61 bg Yuganov
Konstantin/Shutterstock. All
other photographs NASA.

Contents

One Small Step, One Giant Leap

Look up at the Moon in the night sky. Now imagine being the first human to visit the Moon. Its surface is dusty and dry, and you need to wear a special space suit. In the distance, planet Earth looks like a blue marble. But what was it really like to walk on the Moon? And how did the astronauts get there?

On July 20, 1969, astronauts Neil Armstrong and Buzz Aldrin became the first humans to set foot on the Moon. Back on Earth, 530 million people around the world watched on TV as Armstrong and Aldrin explored the Moon.

The Moon landing was like something from a science fiction movie—but this was real! As Neil Armstrong said when he first set foot on the Moon, "That's one small step for [a] man, one giant leap for mankind."

The Moon landing was a dangerous mission. Would the astronauts return to Earth alive?

A Changing World

The year 1969 was full of both excitement and upheaval. It was a time of protests, marches, and calls for peace. People everywhere, especially young people, were standing up for what they believed in.

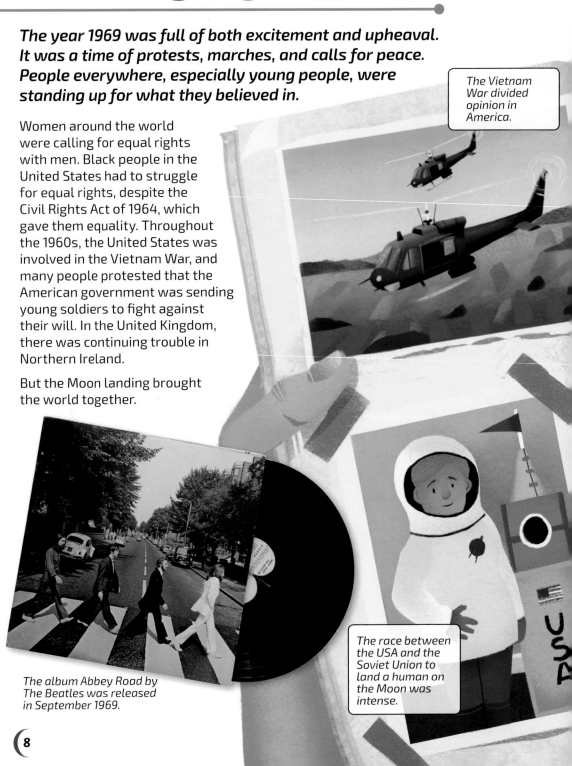

The Vietnam War divided opinion in America.

Women around the world were calling for equal rights with men. Black people in the United States had to struggle for equal rights, despite the Civil Rights Act of 1964, which gave them equality. Throughout the 1960s, the United States was involved in the Vietnam War, and many people protested that the American government was sending young soldiers to fight against their will. In the United Kingdom, there was continuing trouble in Northern Ireland.

But the Moon landing brought the world together.

The album Abbey Road by The Beatles was released in September 1969.

The race between the USA and the Soviet Union to land a human on the Moon was intense.

Non-violent protests against racial discrimination gained national attention.

The Vietnam War lasted from November 1955 to April 1975.

First Human in Space

The United States and the Soviet Union were rivals in world politics, and also in the race to explore space. In 1957, the Soviets launched the first satellite, called Sputnik 1, into space. The United States followed with its own satellite, Explorer. Both countries sent animals into space. The next step would be a human in space.

The Soviets achieved this on April 12, 1961, when cosmonaut Yuri Gagarin blasted into space in Vostok 1. The flight lasted 108 minutes, making one complete orbit around Earth by traveling at speeds of 17,000 miles per hour (27,300 km/h).

The most dangerous part of his mission was coming back to Earth. Gagarin managed to eject from the space capsule and safely parachute down to Earth, where he quickly became an international celebrity.

➲ As the rocket Vostok 1 launched, Gagarin shouted, "Let's go!"

⊙ Yuri Gagarin was on the front page of many newspapers around the world.

Feature Index

	Page		Page
Able	11	Editorials	4
Announcements	4	Sports	27
Comics	25	Society	
Crossword	11	Want Ads	36
Jumble	11	Radio-TV	26

28 PAGES TODAY

The Huntsville Times

VOL. 51, NO. 21   CHICAGO DAILY NEWS SERVICE   HUNTSVILLE, ALABAMA, WEDNESDAY, APR. 12, 1961   ASSOCIATED PRESS – WIREPHOTO

Where Progress...

Covers The Valley!

45c PER WEEK

Man Enters Space

'So Close, Yet So Far,' Sighs Cape

U.S. Had Hoped For Own Launch

CAPE CANAVERAL, Fla. (AP) — The Redstone rocket which the United States had hoped would boost the first man into space stands on a launching pad here. The Soviet Union beat its firing date by at least two weeks.

"So close, yet so far," commented a technician who is helping groom the Redstone to send one of America's astronauts on a short sub-orbital flight, hopefully late this month or early in May.

"If we hadn't had those troubles last fall and on the chimp flight and Little Joe shots this year we might have made it," the technician said.

"But you have to give the Russian scientists credit. They've accomplished a remarkable breakthrough."

Soviet Officer Orbits Globe In 5-Ton Ship

Maximum Height Reached Reported As 188 Miles

MOSCOW (AP)—A Soviet astronaut has orbited the globe for more than an hour and returned safely to receive the plaudits of scientists and political leaders alike. Soviet announcements and U.S. space experts left behind in the contest to put the first man into space.

By the Soviet account, Maj. Yuri Alekseyvich Gagarin, rode a five-ton spaceship once around the earth in an orbit taking an hour and 30 minutes. He was in the air a total of an hour and 48 minutes.

The whole sequence of events and the announcements relating to it raised a number of questions. The Soviet announcement...

VON BRAUN'S REACTION:

To Keep Up, U.S.A.

Hobbs Admits 1944 Slaying

A fault on reentry caused Gagarin's space capsule to spin out of control. The capsule's temperature rose alarmingly.

Gagarin: "I was in a cloud of fire rushing toward Earth."

First spacewoman

Soviet cosmonaut Valentina Tereshkova was chosen for the space program because of her skill as a parachute jumper. In 1963, she became the first woman in space. During her three-day mission in Vostok 6, Tereshkova orbited Earth 48 times.

The Space Race

Only 23 days after Gagarin's historic space flight, Alan Shepard became the first American in space. He flew 116 miles (187 km) high and then returned to Earth in a flight lasting just over 15 minutes.

In May 1961, President John F. Kennedy declared, "I believe that this nation should commit itself to achieving the goal, before this decade is out, of landing a man on the Moon and returning him safely to Earth."

No one knew exactly how to land a man on the Moon, but they had confidence in the potential of technology. After all, the technology of their generation was already incredibly advanced compared with the past.

NASA (National Aeronautics and Space Administration), the American organization in charge of space exploration, had been set up in 1958 with the aim of expanding human knowledge of space. But now NASA focused specifically on exploring the Moon.

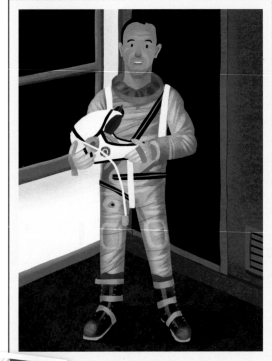

Alan Shepard

Astronaut Alan Shepard became an American hero when he flew to space in the Freedom 7 space capsule in 1961. Shepard returned to space in 1971 and became the fifth person to walk on the Moon. He even hit two golf balls on the Moon and watched them fly away into space.

◉ President Kennedy, his wife Jackie, and Vice President Johnson gathered to watch Alan Shepard's flight into space.

President John F. Kennedy regularly addressed colleagues from all political parties. He never got to see a human land on the Moon, as he was assassinated in November 1963.

Space Missions

Each space mission brought NASA several steps closer to the goal of landing a human on the Moon. One of the first major advances occurred in 1962, when John Glenn became the first American to orbit Earth, traveling around three times in the Friendship 7 Mercury capsule.

Astronaut John Glenn's three orbits around Earth in 1962 lasted almost five hours, a substantial increase over NASA's previous space flights of just over 15 minutes. In 1998, Glenn traveled into space again at the age of 77— the oldest person to take on such a mission.

↥ John Glenn enters his Friendship 7 capsule and is ready to begin his mission.

↦ John Glenn takes photographs during his space mission in 1998.

Apollo 1

In January 1967, the Apollo 1 mission ended in tragedy when the Command Module caught fire during a preflight test. Astronauts Virgil Grissom, Edward White, and Roger Chaffee all died. The disaster led NASA to improve safety precautions.

By 1968, the U.S. space program had come a long way. In October of that year, Apollo 7 orbited Earth continuously for 11 days, and on Christmas Eve, Apollo 8 made the first manned orbit of the Moon.

In March 1969, NASA launched Apollo 9 into space to orbit Earth and practice various tasks, such as testing space suits. In May 1969, the Apollo 10 Lunar Module came within 50,000 feet (just over 15 km) of the Moon's surface, but didn't land.

The preparations were complete, and NASA was now ready for the big event—an Apollo mission to land humans on the Moon.

⊙ Apollo 8's view of Earth and the Moon. Images taken from space changed how people thought of our planet.

Apollo 11 Astronauts

Who would NASA choose to go to the Moon? That was a big question. NASA selected three experienced astronauts— Neil Armstrong, Buzz Aldrin, and Michael Collins.

Neil Armstrong

Mission Commander Neil Armstrong was born in Ohio. He was fascinated by airplanes and earned his pilot's license at age 16—before he could even drive a car. Later, Armstrong became a test pilot, flying high-speed aircraft into space.

⬆ *Aldrin, Armstrong, and Collins on the day after their selection was announced to the public.*

◀ *Neil A. Armstrong, Commander; Michael Collins, Command Module Pilot; and Edwin E. Aldrin Jr., Lunar Module Pilot.*

In 1962, NASA accepted Armstrong into the second class of astronauts it had ever put together. In 1966, he was command pilot for Gemini 8, where he and fellow astronaut David Scott performed the first space docking in orbit—the linking of two space vehicles. But the space vehicles began to spin uncontrollably. Armstrong regained control and was later praised for his quick thinking. He was a skilled astronaut with the qualities needed to lead the mission to the Moon.

❍ Neil Armstrong with his wife, Janet, and two sons: Eric, who was 12 years old at the time of the Moon landing in 1969, and Mark, who was six.

Gemini 8

On March 16, 1966, astronauts Neil Armstrong and David Scott successfully completed their space mission. With the yellow flotation device deployed, their spacecraft landed in the ocean, where the pair awaited rescue. The green dye released on landing helped rescuers spot the craft from the air. Despite having spent almost 11 hours in space, orbiting Earth six times, both astronauts suffered more from seasickness than from their time in space.

Apollo 11 Astronauts

Buzz Aldrin

Lunar Module pilot Edwin E. "Buzz" Aldrin Jr. grew up in New Jersey and served in the Air Force, where he was awarded the Distinguished Flying Cross. He studied techniques for designing and building spacecraft and joined NASA in 1963.

His technique for docking spacecraft in orbit was crucial to the success of NASA's space programs. In 1966, as pilot of the Gemini 12 space mission, Aldrin performed a space walk outside of the vehicle, known as extravehicular activity (EVA).

◐ The first space selfie taken by Aldrin!

◐ It was Aldrin who suggested training underwater to simulate walking in space.

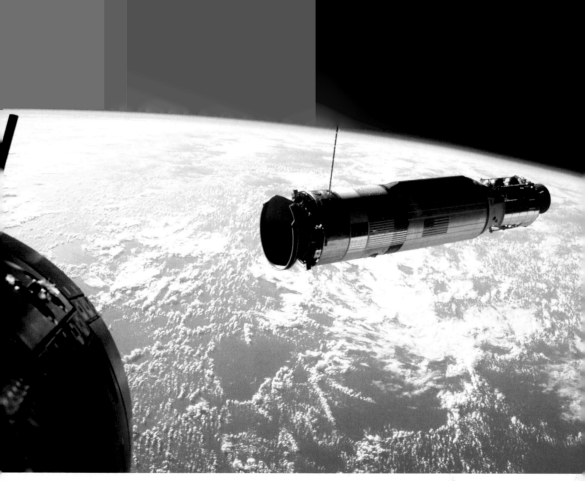

↗ The Gemini spacecraft (left) was piloted by Michael Collins. The other craft, Agena (right), was at the same orbit approach at the same time—known as a rendezvous.

Michael Collins

Command Module pilot Michael Collins was born in Rome, Italy, but grew up in Washington, D.C. He served in the United States Air Force and, like Armstrong, became a test pilot, flying fighter jets.

He was a backup pilot for NASA's Gemini 7 mission in 1963, and pilot for Gemini 10 in 1966. During Gemini 10, Collins docked his spacecraft with two other vehicles in separate locations. He also completed two EVAs, including one particularly tricky space walk during which he recovered an important experiment from one of the other vehicles. The success of this mission added to the knowledge of human space flight.

Shooting for the Moon

It took about 400,000 people doing a wide variety of jobs to get the three Apollo 11 astronauts to the Moon. There were backup astronauts; engineers and mechanics; scientists, seamstresses, doctors, and astronomers; navigators and Mission Control staff, plus managers, secretaries, cleaning and catering staff, and many, many more.

Geologists predicted that the Moon's surface would be similar to rough, rocky craters in Arizona.

Mechanics, **welders**, **electricians**, and others built the spacecraft.

We were incredibly proud of our dads.

Backup astronauts
James Lovell, William Anders, and Fred Haise

Astronauts
Neil Armstrong, Buzz Aldrin, and Michael Collins

We sewed the layers to make the space suits.

As engineers, we designed the spacecraft.

Apollo 11 Mission Patch

The astronauts' names are not on the Apollo 11 patch because NASA wanted to honor everyone involved. The bald eagle is the national symbol of the U.S. It is shown landing on the Moon with an olive branch in its claws to represent peace. Earth is in the background.

I helped develop special freeze-dried food for the astronauts to eat in space.

We were worried our husbands wouldn't come back.

We spoke to the astronauts in space from Mission Control in Houston, Texas.

Air Force General **Samuel C. Phillips** *was in charge of the Apollo Manned Lunar Landing Program.*

Navy diver *who swam to meet the astronauts after splashdown in the Pacific Ocean.*

Photographer *Ralph Morse for LIFE magazine*

Space Suits

The astronauts' space suits had to allow them to move around easily, while also protecting them from dangers on the Moon, such as rocks, extreme temperatures, and the airless atmosphere.

NASA hired a specially trained team of seamstresses at an underwear manufacturer to make the space suits. Each suit had many layers made of different materials. One layer was pressurized with oxygen to allow the astronauts to breath. Some of the materials were invented specially for the space suits—for example, the astronauts wore a piped garment, which kept them cool. Specially developed ribbed space boots allowed the astronauts to walk on the Moon's dust and rocks.

◑ *Neil Armstrong had a "to do" checklist sewn onto the cuff of his space suit.*

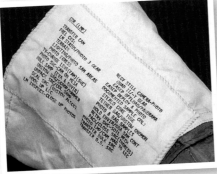

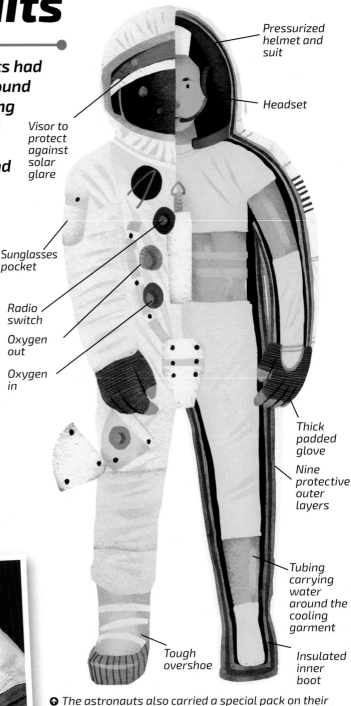

Pressurized helmet and suit

Headset

Visor to protect against solar glare

Sunglasses pocket

Radio switch

Oxygen out

Oxygen in

Thick padded glove

Nine protective outer layers

Tubing carrying water around the cooling garment

Tough overshoe

Insulated inner boot

◐ *The astronauts also carried a special pack on their back containing a Portable Life Support System (PLSS), which supplied them with oxygen, water, and power while they were away from their space vehicle.*

Eleanor Foraker, seamstress: "We made up each layer separately for the whole suit . . . Then we piled them up: one layer on top of another layer."

Space suit tester

The space suit tester was about the same size as the three astronauts, so it was his job to test the space suits and boots. He spent a lot of time walking on a treadmill while engineers studied how well he was able to move in different space suits.

Astronaut Training

How does a person prepare to go to the Moon? The astronauts trained to be in excellent physical condition, but they also practiced every detail of their mission over and over again.

They practiced withstanding g-forces—the increased pull of gravity that they would feel as the rocket soared swiftly out of Earth's atmosphere. (It's similar to how a really fast fairground ride feels, but much, much stronger.) They also practiced walking and moving around in low gravity and carrying out tasks in their new space suits.

⊙ *Astronaut Neil Armstrong practiced various tasks in a simulator.*

⊙ *Buzz Aldrin practiced being in weightless conditions in a specially built plane.*

The astronauts used simulators to practice flying the modules, especially for the tricky maneuver of docking. They carried out the experiments that they would be doing in space, and studied astronomy and geology to learn about the stars and the environment they might find on the Moon. They had to be prepared for everything.

⊙ The astronauts practiced walking at an angle on the Reduced Gravity Walking Simulator. Walking would have a similar feel in reduced gravity on the Moon.

⊙ A simulator called a centrifuge was built to train the astronauts to deal with the g-forces they would experience at launch and on their return to Earth. It would spin exceptionally fast—like a fairground ride.

Apollo 11 Vehicles

The engineers and technicians used everything they had learned from previous space missions when designing the Apollo 11 spacecraft.

Saturn V rocket

During previous Apollo missions, Saturn V had already proved that it was powerful enough to travel beyond Earth's orbit and reach the Moon. For the Apollo 11 mission, the Saturn V rocket had three stages, each with several engines. Each stage dropped off from the rocket once its fuel was used up. At the rocket's nose sat the combined Command Module and Service Module, and the Lunar Module.

Launch Escape System

Command Module

Service Module

Lunar Module

Instrument Unit

Third Stage

Second Stage

Command/ Service Modules

Command Module

Service Module

Crew compartment

Thrusters

Propulsion engine nozzle

Antennae

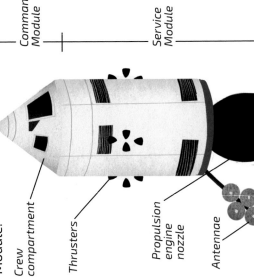

↩ The Instrument Unit is lowered into place on top of the third stage of the

At a total height of 363 feet (111 meters), Saturn V was as tall as a 36-story building. When fully fueled, it weighed 6.2 million pounds (2.8 million kg), about as much as 400 adult elephants. It had the power to launch 130 tons (118,000 kg) into orbit around Earth, or 50 tons (45,300 kg) to the Moon. That's roughly the same as launching ten buses into orbit around Earth, or four buses to the Moon. Launching three astronauts to the Moon should be no problem!

First Stage

Lunar Module

Ascent stage

Descent stage

Antenna

Radar antenna

Thrusters

Ladder

Landing gear

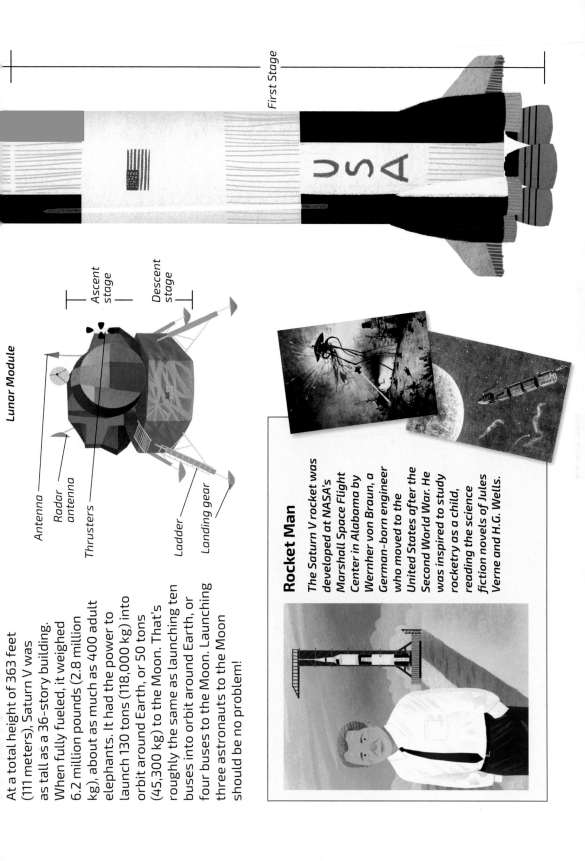

Rocket Man

The Saturn V rocket was developed at NASA's Marshall Space Flight Center in Alabama by Wernher von Braun, a German-born engineer who moved to the United States after the Second World War. He was inspired to study rocketry as a child, reading the science fiction novels of Jules Verne and H.G. Wells.

Apollo 11 Modules

Columbia Command Module

In the Command Module (known as Columbia), the three astronauts were squeezed into roughly the space of a small car—only 10.6 feet (3.2 m) tall by 12.8 feet (3.9 m) at its widest point. They had very little room to move around. Special heat shields on the Command Module protected the astronauts from temperature extremes, especially when reentering Earth's atmosphere on their return.

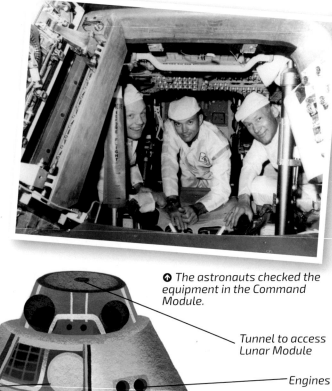

○ The astronauts checked the equipment in the Command Module.

Tunnel to access Lunar Module

Engines

Window

Crew access hatch

Earth landing parachutes

Insulation layer

Outer heat shield

Engines

Outer layer of heat shield

A Service Module providing power and fuel was attached to the Command Module for most of the mission, but was then released. Together they were called the CSM. The Command Module was the only part of the entire spacecraft to return to Earth.

Eagle Lunar Module

What sort of space vehicle could take humans to the Moon's surface and then lift off again to return to Earth? Yet another question that no one had answered before. The engineers had to use their imagination to create the Lunar Module (known as Eagle).

The Module had two sections. The lower descent stage held the landing gear, which would carry out experiments on the Moon, plus a rocket engine to descend to the Moon's surface. The upper ascent stage carried the crew and their equipment, plus a rocket engine to lift off again. At the end of the mission, the lower descent stage acted as a launch pad from the Moon and stayed there. The upper ascent stage docked with the Command Module, after which it was also dropped.

Smaller is better

The notion of a separate Lunar Module was the idea of John Houbolt, an engineer on NASA's Lunar Mission Steering Group. He had to work hard to persuade the other NASA engineers that it would be better than the enormous rocket they had in mind.

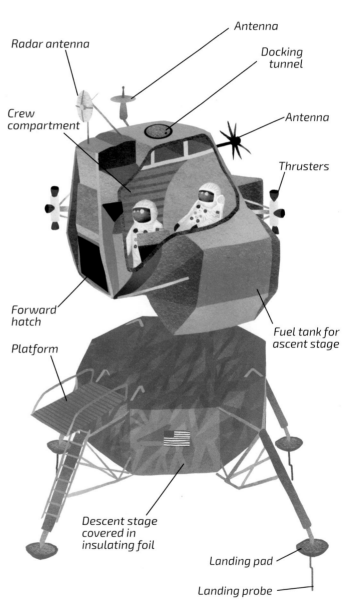

Radar antenna

Antenna

Docking tunnel

Crew compartment

Antenna

Thrusters

Forward hatch

Platform

Fuel tank for ascent stage

Descent stage covered in insulating foil

Landing pad

Landing probe

Human Computers

In the 1960s, computers were only about as powerful as today's handheld calculators. NASA relied on a group of mathematicians known as "human computers" based at Langley Research Center in Virginia.

Katherine Johnson, Mary Jackson, Dorothy Vaughan, and many of the other "human computers" were African-American women. Their extraordinary mathematical skill and hard work were crucial to the success of the space program.

At a time when women and African-Americans were bravely struggling for the same rights as white men, NASA's "human computers" did not receive the credit they deserved.

⊙ The "human computers" were initially hired to help ease the engineers' workload.

◐ Early machine computers weren't as reliable or efficient as the "human computers."

◉ During her time at NASA, Melba Roy Mouton led a group of "human computers" and became Head Computer Programmer.

Using adding machines, pencils, and paper, the mathematicians plotted graphs on the speed of the spacecraft, rotation of Earth, orbit of the Moon around Earth, and other factors in order to calculate the trajectory (flight path) of the spacecraft.

Katherine Johnson

When astronaut John Glenn was preparing for his mission to become the first American to orbit Earth in 1962, he famously only trusted the calculations of aerospace technologist Katherine Johnson, one of the "human computers."

Preparing for Launch

The Apollo 11 rocket launched from the Kennedy Space Center, on the Florida coast. By the late 1960s, about 17,000 people were working at Kennedy Space Center, and as the launch date approached, engineers, technicians, scientists, and other staff checked and tested every detail of the mission. Excitement was building.

The rocket and the modules had been put together at the Vehicle Assembly Building and transported to the launchpad on two giant crawler transporters.

One week before planned liftoff, the Countdown Demonstration Test—the official practice launch—took place. Important challenges and lessons were learned during the test, meaning the official launch was ready. Chief of Pre-Flight Operations Raul E. "Ernie" Reyes confirmed that Apollo 11 was ready to go.

Charlie Mars, Lunar Module project engineer: "We didn't want to go home at night. We just wanted to keep going, and we couldn't wait to get up and get back in the morning—because we're going to the Moon!"

Vehicle Assembly Building

The Vehicle Assembly Building at the Kennedy Space Center had to be big enough to fit the Saturn V rocket inside. It is still one of the largest buildings in the world.

Liftoff

5 . . . 4 . . . 3 . . . 2 . . . 1 . . . Liftoff!

On July 16, 1969, at 9:32 a.m., at the Kennedy Space Center in Florida, the Saturn V rocket launched, with the three astronauts inside. The Apollo 11 space mission was headed for the Moon!

With an enormous roar, the Saturn V rocket approached the speed of sound just one minute into the flight.

About 500 people worked the controls in the Firing Room of the Kennedy Space Center, while about 5,000 others provided support.

Astronauts Armstrong, Aldrin, and Collins sat in the Command Module at the nose of the Saturn V rocket. They soared through Earth's atmosphere and into space, dropping the first two rocket stages as they used up fuel. At 115 miles (185 km) above Earth, they began orbiting, and the crew checked the spacecraft systems were performing well. Halfway through the second orbit of Earth, the last rocket stage sent them toward the Moon!

⊙ *Around one million spectators on the ground watched the launch. The noise was deafening!*

Mission Control

At Mission Control in Houston, Texas, flight controllers monitored all aspects of Apollo 11's flight. Teams worked in shifts so Mission Control was fully staffed. Backup teams were also on call.

Mission Control kept the Apollo 11 mission running as smoothly as possible. Flight controllers monitored the systems in the rocket and modules. They checked the oxygen levels and other crucial supplies for the astronauts. They ensured that the astronauts' vital statistics, such as body temperature, pulse, and breathing rate, were at safe levels.

Mission Control also communicated with the astronauts. The CapCom (Capsule Communicator) relayed messages between the astronauts in space and the controllers on the ground. It was a very important job.

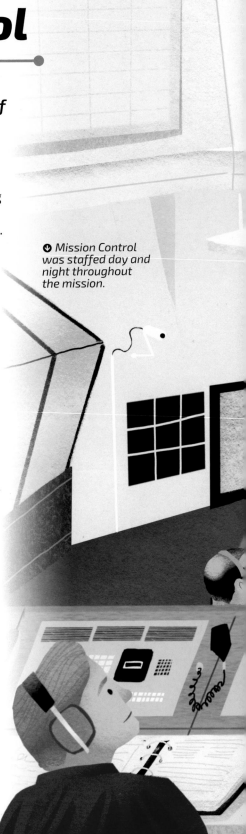

⊙ Mission Control was staffed day and night throughout the mission.

Communication to the capsule

CapCom Charlie Duke was also a trained astronaut. In 1972, he landed on the Moon as Lunar Module pilot with Apollo 16.

Life in Space

The Apollo 11 astronauts spent eight days in space.
Where did they sleep? What did they eat?
And how did they go to the bathroom?

The astronauts had to be strapped in to sleep or else they would float around in the low gravity in space. It wasn't very comfortable, especially as they were squashed inside the small space modules.

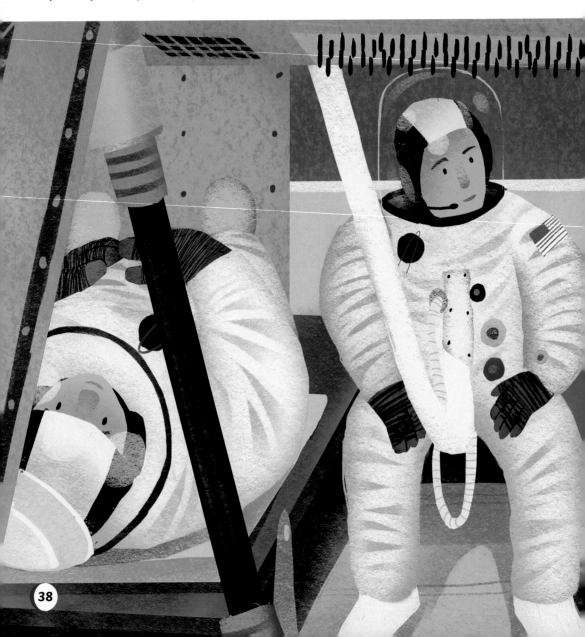

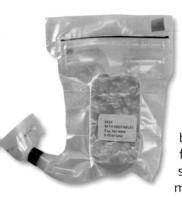

Scientists had developed freeze-dried food that was lightweight and easy to store in bags on board. The astronauts squirted droplets of water from a special spigot into the food bag and kneaded it like bread for a few minutes. Then they squeezed the food into their mouth to eat.

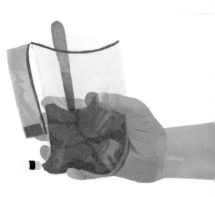

As for toilets, they don't work in space because everything would float! The astronauts used special devices that collected their body waste. They also had special diaper-style linings inside their space suits.

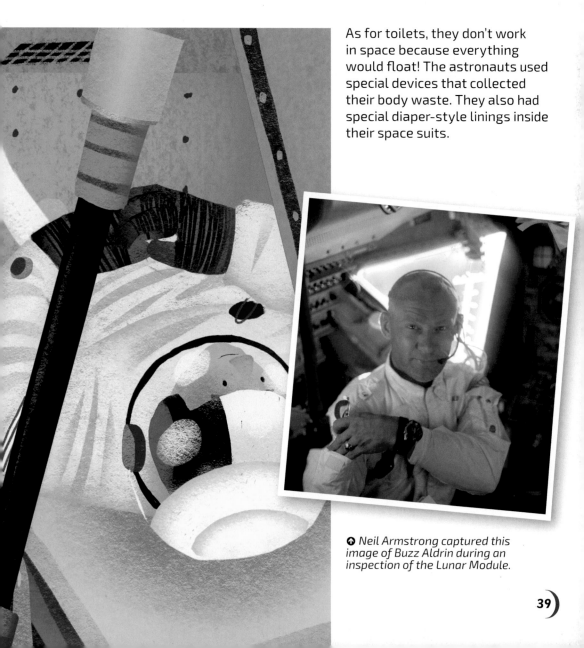

⬆ Neil Armstrong captured this image of Buzz Aldrin during an inspection of the Lunar Module.

Almost There . . .

The three stages of the rocket had dropped away some time ago. Now the Command and Service Module (CSM), with the Lunar Module on the back, orbited the Moon twelve times, with the astronauts studying it as they flew around.

During the thirteenth orbit, the Lunar Module (Eagle) separated from the CSM, the first of many maneuvers never attempted before. As Armstrong and Aldrin prepared to try and land the Lunar Module on the Moon, Collins continued to orbit the Moon in the CSM.

➔ The Lunar Module separated from the Command and Service Moduleand headed toward the Moon's surface.

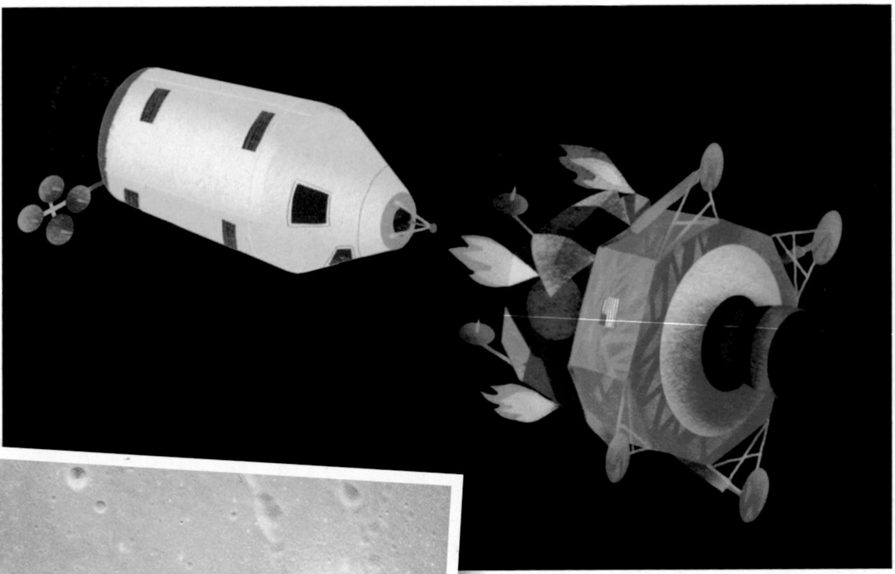

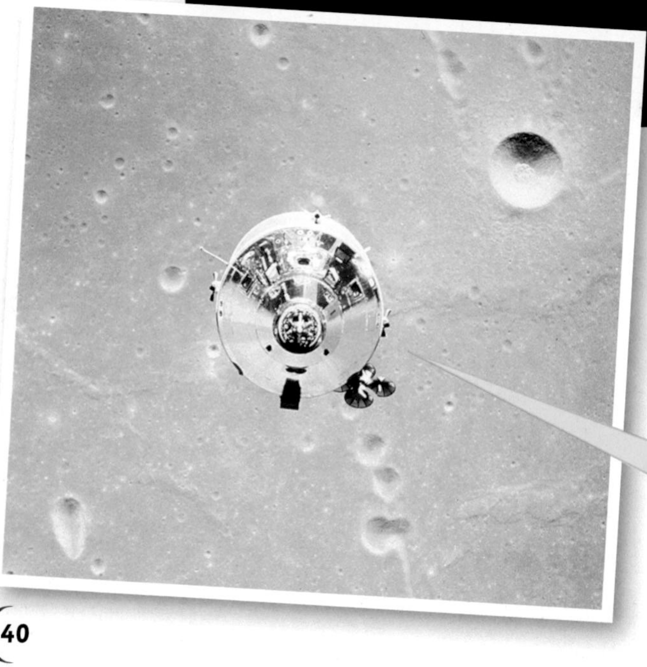

➔ Once Armstrong and Aldrin flew off in the Lunar Module, Collins was left on his own in the CSM, in the vast emptiness of space.

Collins: "I was alone in a way that no earthling has ever been before."

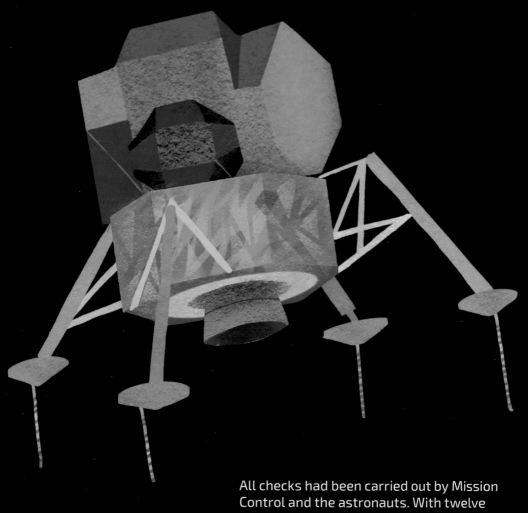

All checks had been carried out by Mission Control and the astronauts. With twelve minutes' worth of fuel remaining, it was time to land on the Moon. The Lunar Module began to descend to about 10 miles (16 km) above the Moon. Would there be enough fuel? Would humans finally land on the Moon?

Moon Landing

As the Lunar Module descended toward the surface of the Moon, alarms sounded. Code 1202, and then a 1201! What was the problem?

At Mission Control, Steve Bales, controller for guidance and navigation, and Jack Garman, a software expert, recalled when similar alarms had gone off during a practice liftoff. Flight Director Gene Kranz had them write down what every alarm meant. Now they checked their list and realized there was no need to worry.

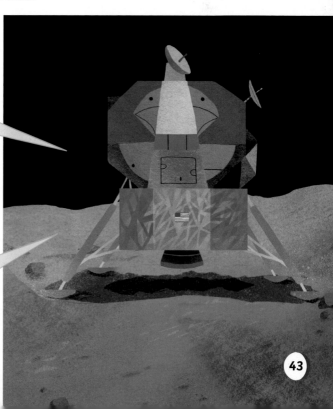

The Eagle has landed! Four days after liftoff, the Lunar Module finally touched down on the Moon.

Margaret Hamilton

Software engineer Margaret Hamilton was leader of the team that designed the software system on the Lunar Module. When the alarms sounded, the software was able to prioritize tasks so that Apollo 11 could continue its mission.

Dealing with the alarms had used up time and precious fuel. The astronauts had to land quickly or the Lunar Module would run out of fuel and crash onto the Moon's surface.

But landing wasn't easy. There was a crater and a field of boulders in the way. With less than 30 seconds of fuel left, Armstrong landed the Lunar Module safely on the Moon in a location known as Tranquility Base.

Armstrong: "Tranquility Base here. The Eagle has landed."

Mission Control: "Roger, Tranquility. Be advised there's lots of smiling faces in this room, and all over the world."

Armstrong: "There are two of them up here."

Collins: "And don't forget one in the Command Module."

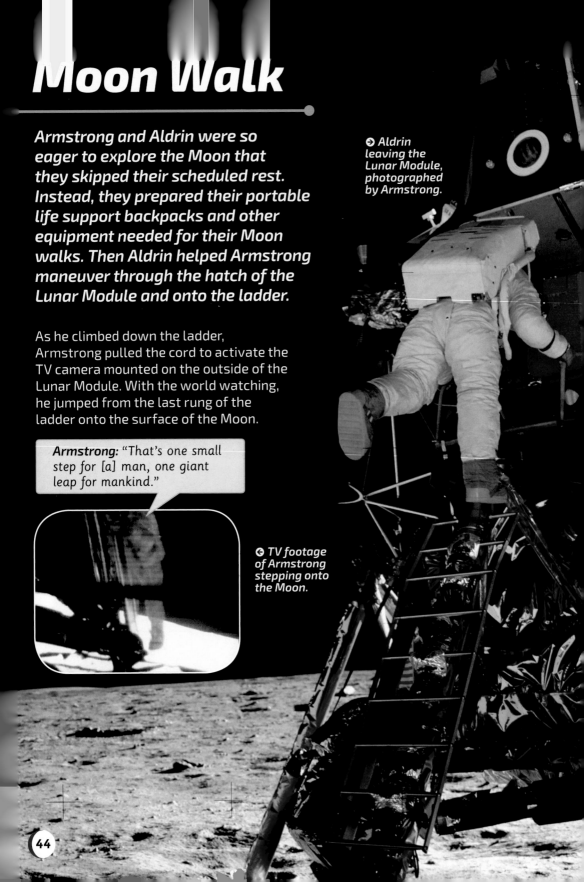

Moon Walk

Armstrong and Aldrin were so eager to explore the Moon that they skipped their scheduled rest. Instead, they prepared their portable life support backpacks and other equipment needed for their Moon walks. Then Aldrin helped Armstrong maneuver through the hatch of the Lunar Module and onto the ladder.

As he climbed down the ladder, Armstrong pulled the cord to activate the TV camera mounted on the outside of the Lunar Module. With the world watching, he jumped from the last rung of the ladder onto the surface of the Moon.

Armstrong: "That's one small step for [a] man, one giant leap for mankind."

→ *Aldrin leaving the Lunar Module, photographed by Armstrong.*

← *TV footage of Armstrong stepping onto the Moon.*

Aldrin: "The surface is fine and powdery . . . I can kick it up loosely with my toe."

⊙ *Buzz Aldrin took photographs of his footprints on the Moon's talcum-like surface.*

Twenty minutes later, Aldrin also stepped onto the Moon. The two astronauts walked and jumped around in low gravity. Aldrin called the Moon "magnificent desolation," meaning that it was beautiful, but lifeless.

Working on the Moon

One of the astronauts' main tasks was to take photos and film footage of the Moon. Armstrong took most of the photographs, so the pictures were mainly of Aldrin.

Armstrong and Aldrin collected more than 47 lb (21 kg) of rocks and other samples from the Moon. They conducted experiments, including one on Moonquakes and another on wind from the Sun. They also set up Laser Ranging Retroreflectors, which would help measure the distance between Earth and the Moon by reflecting lasers sent from large telescopes on Earth.

Armstrong and Aldrin spent about two and half hours on the Moon. They left behind an American flag, goodwill messages from 73 different countries, medallions honoring the Apollo 1 astronauts and Soviet cosmonauts who had died on space missions, and a plaque commemorating their visit to the Moon.

⊻ *Aldrin conducted several experiments.*

⬆ *A photograph showing Aldrin, the Lunar Module, and equipment used to take measurements and collect samples.*

HERE MEN FROM THE PLANET EARTH
FIRST SET FOOT UPON THE MOON
JULY 1969, A. D.
WE CAME IN PEACE FOR ALL MANKIND

MICHAEL COLLINS
ASTRONAUT

EDWIN E. ALDRIN, JR.
ASTRONAUT

RICHARD NIXON
PRESIDENT, UNITED STATES OF AMERICA

The plaque that Armstrong and Aldrin left on the Moon says, "Here men from the planet Earth first set foot upon the Moon July 1969, A.D. We came in peace for all mankind."

The World Watched

About 530 million people around the world watched the Moon walks on TV. Enormous satellite dishes in the Australian outback received signals from the television camera on the Moon. The TV signals were relayed to the city of Sydney, Australia, and then to Mission Control in Houston, Texas, and then around the world.

In most of the United States, it was late at night. People stayed up so they wouldn't miss the Moon walk, and many woke their children to witness the historic event. Some people gathered to watch together. In New York City, a "moon-in" event was held in Central Park, where people watched the events live on large screens.

◀ *Honeysuckle Creek, Australia, was the first site to receive signals from the Moon and relay them to the viewers watching.*

Expert reporting

British astronomer Sir Patrick Moore reported on the Moon landing. He was an expert in mapping the Moon, and NASA used his research to prepare for Apollo 11.

In Europe, it was early morning of the next day. Teachers brought TV sets into classrooms to watch with their students. How amazing that people were really walking on the Moon—that big rock in space that we see in the night sky!

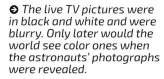
The live TV pictures were in black and white and were blurry. Only later would the world see color ones when the astronauts' photographs were revealed.

Back to Earth

It was time for Armstrong and Aldrin to rejoin Collins in the Command and Service Module. This was one of the trickiest parts of the mission. President Richard Nixon even had a speech prepared in case the astronauts didn't make it home.

Armstrong and Aldrin fired up the ascent stage of the Lunar Module and lifted off. Exactly as planned, they docked with the CSM as it flew past. The Lunar Module was disconnected once all of the three astronauts were safely inside the Command Module. The Service Module was then released. The 250,000-mile (400,000-km) journey back to Earth had begun.

⊙ *Back in the Lunar Module, Aldrin and Armstrong are tired, but elated.*

⊙ *Michael Collins (inside the Command Module) took this photograph of the Lunar Module just before it docked with the CSM.*

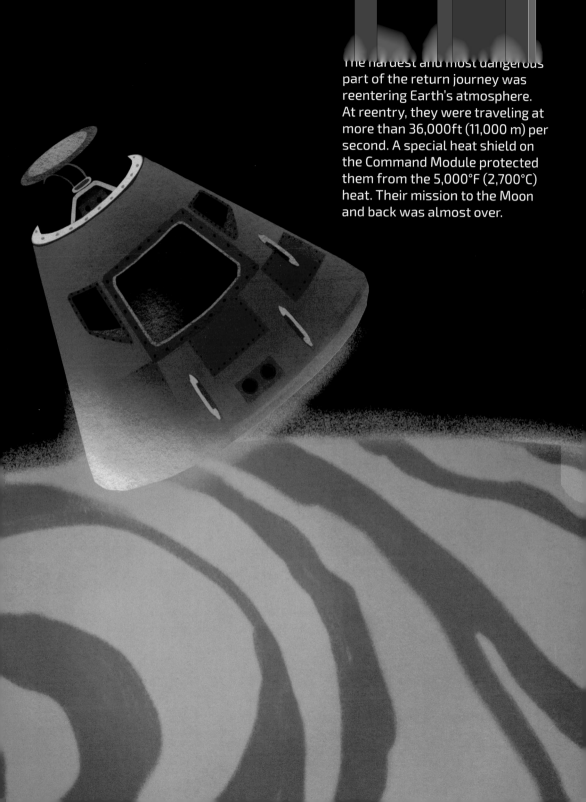

The hardest and most dangerous part of the return journey was reentering Earth's atmosphere. At reentry, they were traveling at more than 36,000ft (11,000 m) per second. A special heat shield on the Command Module protected them from the 5,000°F (2,700°C) heat. Their mission to the Moon and back was almost over.

Splashdown

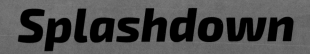

The Command Module was on target for splashdown in the Pacific Ocean. At about 10,000 ft (3,000 m) above the ocean, specially designed parachutes opened and the Command Module drifted down into the water. Recovery helicopters flew over from the nearby USS Hornet aircraft carrier. The astronauts had made it back to Earth.

We're OK!

John Wolfram was one of four divers from the U.S. Navy who swam out to anchor the Command Module after splashdown. He said, "I looked in the hatch window to see if the astronauts were OK. They smiled and gave me a thumbs-up."

◉ *After splashdown, the now famous Command Module was put on display in the National Air and Space Museum, in Washington, D.C.*

The astronauts were immediately put into quarantine away from anyone else, even their families, so they wouldn't spread any unknown germs.

After almost a month in quarantine, Armstrong, Aldrin, and Collins were finally able to join the world's celebrations of the Moon landing. There were parades, a meeting with the president, and a lot of interviews. Everyone wanted to hear their stories and experiences.

Apollo 11 facts

Departure: July 16, 1969

Arrival on the Moon: July 20, 1969

Moon walk (EVA): 2 hours, 30 minutes

Total time on the Moon: 21 hours, 36 minutes

Return to Earth: July 24, 1969

Duration of mission: 8 days, 3 hours, 18 minutes, 35 seconds

Total distance: 953,054 miles (1.53 million km)

Amazing Memories

Do you know anyone who remembers watching the astronauts land on the Moon? Here are a few memories from those who were watching from all over the world.

Molly Wolfe, Yorkshire, U.K.
"I was 12 years old when I watched the Moon landing from the sofa in my grandmother's living room. We were watching on television and I remember clearly the beautiful vision of Earth from the Moon and thinking it was something magical. When Armstrong stepped out and did the funny Moon walk, it felt like sci-fi! I also recall thinking it was quite funny that they put up the flag on such an empty landscape."

Bill Coon, Minnesota
"I was 17 and a little nervous about the future. That summer, we had a meeting of the school council at the home of one of our teachers. We were all discussing ideas for the following school year when suddenly we stared in amazement at the small TV screen. Science fiction melded into reality right before our eyes. Humans were walking on the Moon! Anything now seemed possible and the future became more exciting than scary. The Moon landing represented hope."

Mark Leonard, East Anglia, U.K.
"I was 8. What I remember is hearing one lady in our village say that she thought the Moon wasn't as bright since the astronauts had landed, and she was really annoyed about that!"

Enrique A. Farrarons, Philippines
"I was 20 when I watched the Moon landing. I immediately thought, "When can I go to the Moon?" I also wondered where humans would go next. After all, there's a whole universe out there."

Iris Purcell, New York City
"I wondered if the Moon landing had been faked. At 24, I had been protesting against the Vietnam War, and I didn't trust the American government. I was among a group of skeptics who thought that the Moon landing might have been a hoax to boost morale in the country."

Space Technology

Did you know that some everyday items that we now take for granted came about as a result of the Apollo 11 mission to the Moon?

These are just a few of the advances made to everyday life, thanks to Apollo 11.

Cordless power tools were first invented so the astronauts could drill for samples on the Moon.

Modern computer chips that we use in cell phones and other devices were developed using technology from the computer circuits on the Apollo modules.

When you're running and jumping around in your sneakers, imagine the astronauts doing the same thing in their space boots! Modern athletic shoes use cushioned soles that were originally developed for the space boots worn by Armstrong and Aldrin to walk on the Moon.

A Future in Space

Humans have continued to explore space. In 2019, China landed a rover on the side of the Moon that never faces Earth—the first spacecraft ever to do so.

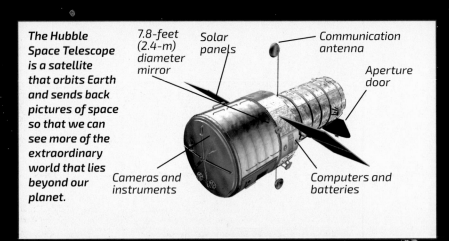

The Hubble Space Telescope is a satellite that orbits Earth and sends back pictures of space so that we can see more of the extraordinary world that lies beyond our planet.

7.8-feet (2.4-m) diameter mirror

Solar panels

Communication antenna

Aperture door

Cameras and instruments

Computers and batteries

Robotic devices called probes are also sent to explore space. These probes can withstand the conditions without risking human life. One such probe is the Mars rover Curiosity, which explores the surface of Mars, the closest planet to Earth.

The International Space Station has been orbiting Earth since 1998. Astronauts stay on the space station for months at a time to conduct experiments.

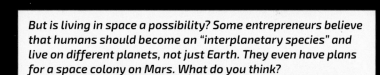

But is living in space a possibility? Some entrepreneurs believe that humans should become an "interplanetary species" and live on different planets, not just Earth. They even have plans for a space colony on Mars. What do you think?

Do You Have What It Takes?

Some important qualities when working in space exploration are curiosity and enthusiasm, the ability to work well with a team, and the persistence to keep trying. Take this quiz to find out about some more qualities needed for different jobs involved in space exploration.

1 Which do you prefer?
- **a** Going on a school field trip
- **b** Organizing a group project
- **c** Building a model rocket
- **d** Doing a science experiment

2 At school, do you usually:
- **a** Listen closely and follow instructions
- **b** Try to do several things at the same time
- **c** Sometimes come up with unusual ideas
- **d** Ask a lot of questions

3 Which is your idea of fun?
- **a** Exploring a new place
- **b** Playing a computer game
- **c** Drawing a picture of a race car
- **d** Going to a science museum

4 Which word best describes you?
- **a** Adventurous
- **b** Organized
- **c** Creative
- **d** Inquisitive

If you've answered mostly . . .

a You love adventures and exploring new places. You're also brave and physically fit. Why not become an astronaut and explore space? You'll need to follow instructions from Mission Control, but at the same time, you've got to be resourceful and quick-thinking so you can solve any problems that occur in space.

b You're good at organizing and working on different things at the same time, but you also have a good eye for detail. You have an air of authority, meaning that people pay attention to what you say. That's important for someone working in Mission Control. How about it?

c You like vehicles and building things and knowing how things work. Would you like to design and build spacecraft and space probes? You'll need to be practical with good technical knowledge, and have the imagination to create spacecraft and probes suitable for exploring different places in space.

d The more you learn about the universe, the more you realize there is to learn. You're focused, precise, and patient. You're also good at finding links between ideas. You could be a space scientist, thinking up experiments for the astronauts to do in space and then analyzing the results.

Glossary

Atmosphere The layer of gases that surround Earth and are held there by gravity. Earth's atmosphere is made up of nitrogen, oxygen, argon, carbon dioxide, and small traces of other gases.

Command Module Also known as Columbia. The part of the Apollo 11 spacecraft where the astronauts lived. This part of the spacecraft returned to Earth with the astronauts inside. It had special heat shields to protect the astronauts from high temperatures.

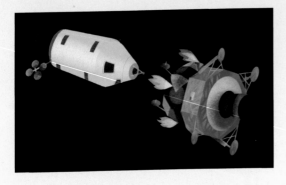

Docking When two separate space vehicles link together in flight. This is a tricky maneuver, as it requires the vehicles to find each other in space and get close enough to join up.

Extravehicular Activity (EVA) Activity that happens outside of the spacecraft, such as a spacewalk.

G-force An increased pull of gravity that astrounauts feel when they are launched out of Earth's atmosphere. It's similar to how it feels on a rollercoaster, but much stronger.

Gravity The force that pulls objects toward each other. It keeps the planets in orbit around the Sun and keeps people and other objects grounded on Earth. The Moon has very low gravity, so astronauts have to learn how to walk and move around in reduced gravity conditions.

Hubble Space Telescope (HST) A space telescope above Earth's atmosphere. It completes a full orbit of Earth every 97 minutes, sending images of planets, stars, and galaxies back to scientists and astronomers on Earth.

International Space Station (ISS) A spacecraft orbiting Earth. Launched in 1998, astronauts live and work on the ISS, carrying out tests and research.

Laser Ranging Retroreflectors Equipment used to measure the distance between the Earth and the Moon. Lasers on the Earth were pointed at retroreflectors on the Moon and the distance between the two can then be calculated.

Lunar Module Also known as the Eagle. A space vehicle, used in the Apollo 11 mission. Neil Armstrong and Buzz Aldrin landed the Lunar Module on the Moon in July 1969.

Mission Control A facility based on Earth that monitors all aspects of a space mission.

Moonquake A shaking sensation (a quake) that occurs on the Moon. Moonquakes last longer but are weaker than earthquakes.

NASA National Aeronautics and Space Administration. An American organization in charge of space exploration. Founded in 1958, NASA was responsible for the first manned mission to the Moon, the Apollo 11.

Orbit The circular path an object takes in space around another object. For example, Earth is in orbit around the Sun, and the Moon is in orbit around Earth.

Portable Life Support System (PLSS) A special pack astronauts carried on their back, which

supplied them with oxygen, water, and power when they were away from their space vehicle.

Probes An unmanned spacecraft that travels through space to collect information. Sputnik 1 was the first probe in space.

Rendezvous When two spacecraft are in the same orbit at the same time and come within a very close distance of each other.

Satellite A satellite is an object that is in orbit. The Moon is a natural satellite, but sometimes artificial satellites are launched into space to do a certain job, such as taking and sending pictures and mapping planets.

Service Module The part of the Apollo 11 spacecraft that provided power, storage, and other important functions needed on the mission. It was connected to the Command Module and was released before landing and did not return to Earth.

Trajectory The path an objects takes through space.

Index